CRYSTAL

S

FOR

CLEANSE

K.C. Hardaway | E. Ramirez

HardawayCo.com

INTRODUCTION

The word crystal comes from the Greek word **kryos**, which means "icy cold". For a long time, rock crystal was described to be ice that had frozen hard forever. Crystals are attractive rock formations that have surprised humans for so many years. They are used for many different purposes, not just for ornament. Myriad of the first radios ever innovated used crystals to transmit the radio waves. Some watches, like quartz watches, still use crystals to this day. They have always been seen as something of beauty and are still often placed with diamonds or other stones inside pieces of jewelry. The majority of crystals now are man-made in laboratories. They are extremely rare to find in the Earth. As you read through this book, you will be able to understand everything about Crystals you need to know.

CHAPTER ONE

USE THE POWERS OF CRYSTAL HEALING

What Are Crystals?

Crystals are solid substances in which the atoms are arranged in regular patterns. Atoms are the tiny building blocks that all things are made from. Almost all minerals are made of crystals. Crystals usually have flat surfaces called faces, and sharp edges. Millions of tiny crystals can cluster together to make a chunk of rock. A crystal's shape is known as its habit. For example, salt crystals are like tiny cubes, zircon crystals (used in jewellery) are like pyramids, while asbestos grows in long strands. There are crystals all around us. Some of the most beautiful crystals, such as rubies and emeralds, can be cut and polished into valuable gems.

How Crystals Are Formed

If you want to see how crystals are formed, you can do a little project in your very own kitchen and see the formation of the crystals occur with your own eyes. This can be done by putting a small amount of table salt into some regular tap water, wait 24 hours, and you will see nice cubed formations. This happens because the water is evaporating, which causes the atoms that make up the salt (the mineral) and the water to come closer together. They will eventually make a nice little uniform cluster of atoms. The more they can come together, the more of a formation will be visible to the naked eye. Scientists can determine what mineral they are looking at by how the crystals form.

Not all crystals form in water. Some crystals can be formed in an element named carbon. Nevertheless, all crystal form the same way, atoms come together and become a uniformed cluster. The process can take as little as a few days to maybe a thousand years. Natural crystals that come from the Earth form the same way. These crystals were formed over a million years ago inside the Earth's crust. They occur when the liquid in the Earth consolidates and the temperature chills. Other crystals form when the liquid makes its way through the clefts and dispense minerals into the clefts.

Examples of Crystals

Examples of everyday materials you encounter as crystals are table salt (sodium chloride or halite crystals), sugar (sucrose), and snowflakes. Many gemstones are crystals, including quartz and diamond.

There are also many materials that resemble crystals but are actually polycrystals. Polycrystals form when microscopic crystals fuse together to form a solid. These materials do not consist of ordered lattices. Examples of polycrystals include ice, many metal samples, and ceramics. Even less structure is displayed by amorphous solids, which have disordered internal structure. An example of an amorphous solid is glass, which may resemble a crystal when faceted, yet isn't one.

Healing Crystals

Only naturally occurring crystals can be used in healing. Although beautiful, man-made crystals such as Austrian and lead crystals lack the vibrational qualities that mean they are able to interact with and benefit us. Many types of crystal are formed in the earth's surface or underground; some are created through sedimentation and built up of many tiny layers. Crystal such as tektite and moldavite are believed to be of extra-terrestrial origin either as meteorites or due to reactions in the earth when a meteorite crashes.

Although science still struggles to fully explain the power of crystals, humans have long been aware that they held the power to focus, transmit, transform and store energy. Crystal healing can also be used with pets, either directly or by placing crystals in their beds or cages. For cats and dogs small crystal charms can also be attached to their collars.

Chemical Bonds in Crystals

The types of chemical bonds formed between atoms or groups of atoms in crystals depend on their size and electronegativity. There are four categories of crystals as grouped by their bonding:

1. **Covalent Crystals** - Atoms in covalent crystals are linked by covalent bonds. Pure nonmetals form covalent crystals (e.g., diamond) as do covalent compounds (e.g., zinc sulfide).

2. **Molecular Crystals** - Entire molecules are bonded to each other in an organized manner. A good example is a sugar crystal, which contains sucrose molecules.

3. **Metallic Crystals** - Metals often form metallic crystals, where some of the valence electrons are free to move throughout the

lattice. Iron, for example, can form different metallic crystals.

4. **Ionic Crystals** - Electrostatic forces form ionic bonds. A classic example is a halite or salt crystal.

What Are Chakras?

Some persons have heard the term chakra on many occasions and have wondered what exactly is it referring to? You cannot see your chakras with your naked eye so it is a bit more difficult to understand what exactly they are. Some intuitive people can see chakras though through their third eye vision but most people can't see them on themselves or anybody else. So what are chakras & how do they affect your life?

Chakras, which mean wheel or disk in Sanskrit, are vital energy centers that can be found along the spine. They connect your body, mind, and spirit. There are seven main chakras, which align the spine, starting from the base of the spine through to the crown of the head. To visualize a chakra in the body, imagine a swirling wheel of energy where matter and consciousness meet. This invisible energy, called *Prana*, is vital life force, which keeps us vibrant, healthy, and alive.

The Importance of the Main Chakras in the Body

These swirling wheels of energy correspond to massive nerve centers in the body. Each of the seven main chakras contains bundles of nerves and major organs as well as our psychological, emotional, and spiritual states of being. Since everything is moving, it's essential that our seven main chakras stay open, aligned, and fluid. If there is a blockage, energy cannot flow. Think of something as simple as your bathtub drain. If you allow too much hair to go into the drain, the bathtub will back up with water, stagnate and eventually bacteria and mold will grow. So is too with our bodies and the chakras. A bathtub is simple; it's physical so the fix is easy.

Keeping a chakra open is a bit more of a challenge, but not so difficult when you have awareness. Since mind, body, soul, and spirit are intimately connected, awareness of an imbalance in one area will help bring the others back into balance. Take for example, a wife, who has recently lost her husband. She develops acute bronchitis, which remains in the chest, and then gets chest pains each time she coughs. The whole heart chakra is affected in this case. If she realizes the connection between the loss and the bronchitis, healing will occur much faster if she honors the grieving process and treats that as well as the physical ailment.

The 7 Chakras and their functions

1st Chakra – Root Chakra

This chakra has to do with how you are here on this earth. It is your most physical chakra and has to do with your survival needs such as food, shelter and financial security. The root chakra also has to do with your physical groundedness, pain, pleasure and your connection to mother earth. If this chakra is imbalanced you will experience things such as constipation, eating disorders, inability to focus or sit still, fears, knee and bone disorders. Anything from the base of the spine down will be affected by this chakra. When the root chakra is in balance you don't worry about your basic needs such as money, food and shelter as you know they will be met. You feel very secure and looked after by the universe.

2nd Chakra – Sacral Chakra

This chakra has to do with your creativity, emotions and sexuality. If this chakra is imbalanced you may be overly emotional and have unnatural attachments to people or things, participate in promiscuous behavior, have a low libido, abdominal cramps, depression and lack of creativity. When the sacral chakra is in balance you have no trouble allowing your creativity to flow. You have no problem with intimacy and are very level headed.

3rd Chakra – Solar Plexus

This chakra has to do with your vitality and self-esteem. The people you chose to hang out with, how you eat and how you see yourself are all effected by this chakra. An imbalanced solar plexus can cause self-esteem and confidence issues, abdominal and digestive issues, ego and personal power issues. If the solar plexus is in balance you have self-confidence in everything you do and you stand up for what you believe is right.

4th Chakra – Heart Chakra

This chakra has to do with love and support. It has to do with how much love you give out and take in because there needs to be a balance of both. You can't only give and not receive because you would not be a balanced individual and that can create problems. If this chakra is imbalanced you can get heart issues such as heart palpitations, chest pain, heart attacks, shallow breathing and needy behaviors.

If the heart chakra is in balance you give and receive love freely therefore having a balance between both. You feel supported by the universe in everything you do furthermore you have respect for all living creatures and people around you.

5th Chakra – Throat Chakra

This chakra has to do with communication and speaking your truth. If it is imbalanced you have trouble speaking up, you may get sore throats, stiff neck and shoulders. If the throat chakra is in balance you are able to clearly communicate and ask for what you want. You have no problem speaking your truth to anyone.

6th Chakra – Third Eye Chakra

This chakra has to do with your intuition and seeing beyond what your physical senses can see. If it is imbalanced you can get eye issues, headaches and nightmares. If the third eye chakra is balanced you have great intuition, are able to see clearly and you get great insight from your spirit guides and angels as you are in higher states of consciousness.

7th Chakra – Crown Chakra

This chakra is associated with your belief systems and your awareness of oneness with higher power. If it is imbalanced you experience things such as depression, limiting beliefs, boredom or confusion. If the crown chakra is in balance, you feel oneness with the universe and everyone around you. You know that we are all one and that no one is separate. You experience clarity and your beliefs align with what you want.

How Crystals and Chakras Interact

Crystals are one of the most important tools for chakra healing. They help to promote energy balance in the body that leads to physical, emotional and spiritual well-being. Each crystal has its own vibrational frequency, just as each chakra does. By choosing crystals that resonate at the same frequencies as each of the chakras, you can remove energy blockages in the chakras and cleanse and rejuvenate them.

You might liken this process to piano tuning, in which case a tuning fork is set to a certain length and struck to cause a vibration that creates a specific sound. Then, the piano key can be matched to the same frequency of the tuning fork, bringing the key into balance. When you use healing stones for chakra healing, your chakras are able to come back into resonance with the frequency they are meant to vibrate at just like the keys on the piano.

The easiest way to balance the chakras is to match the color of the stone with the chakra, although there are exceptions, such as rose quartz, which is pink but helps balance the heart chakra, which is green.

4 Ways to Use Crystals for Chakra Healing

There are four highly effective strategies for balancing the chakras with crystals. All of them are extremely simple. The crystals do all the work, and all you really need to do is be in their presence.

1) Place Chakra Stones Directly on the Body in Line With the Chakras

To do this, lie down and arrange the healing stones along your chakras by color and/or meaning to address your intent. Start with the root chakra and work your way up to encourage the flow of energy.

2) Rest Near Chakra Crystals

Place healing stones under your pillow while sleeping or next to you as you are resting. In many cases, you will feel their energy impacting your mind, body and spirit just by being in their presence.

3) Meditate With Healing Stones

When we meditate with crystals, we enhance our practice and achieve deeper states of consciousness. You might choose to meditate next to a large amethyst geode or you can simply hold small tumbled stones in your hand or place chakra stones on your body in the corresponding position of each chakra.

While you meditate, envision the color of each healing stone doing its work, opening and rejuvenating each chakra, starting at the root chakra and working your way up. If there are specific symptoms you are experiencing as a result of your chakras being blocked, or if there are certain outcomes you want to achieve by cleansing each chakra, then envision those intentions as you meditate. This will further enhance your results.

4) Wear Crystals

The more time you spend with your crystals, the more their frequencies will balance your personal energy field to provide chakra healing. That's why wearing them or keeping them with you at all times is suggested. You can place tumbled stones in your pocket or you can where crystal jewelry, such as a choker necklace for the throat chakra or a longer necklace for the heart chakra.

THE PINEAL GLAND

The term "Pineal Gland" refers to a endocrine gland, residing between the left and right hemispheres of the brain. It resembles a pine cone, hence the name. Seventeenth century philosopher and scientist René Descartes called it the "principal seat of the soul" . The Pineal Gland is the point of connection between the intellect and the body. It is the only section of the brain that exists as a single part rather than one-half of a pair. Because a person never has "more than one thought at a time," – external stimuli is united within the brain before being considered by the soul.

What Does the Pineal Gland Do?

It's a light-activated gland, acting & constructed as a primitive eye. It governs our biorhythms, working w/ other glands to direct our thirst, hunger, sexual desires, biological clock, while synching up energy vibrations in our environment to adjust our circadian rhythm. On the spiritual level, the pineal gland is our third eye -that can be activated to inner and outer world frequencies, enabling one to achieve a sense of all knowing, godlike euphoria and oneness. A pineal gland once tuned into these frequencies with the help of crystals, meditation, yoga or various esoteric methods – enables a person to travel into other dimensions, known as astral travel, astral projection and remote viewing.

On the physical level, the pineal gland creates meletonin, controlling biological rhythms and reproduction hormones. It has an impact on your circadian rhythms – these rhythms are your 24-hour biological cycle characterized by sleep-wake patterns. The pineal gland's full purpose is still a bit of a mystery to the scientific World. There are a variety of crystals that may be used to activate the pineal gland, examples of these would be Copper, Diamond, Gold, Halite, Malachite, Milky Quartz, Sugilite, Silver and Zircon.

Using Crystals for astral projection

Astral traveling is when your astral body leaves your physical body. It is also known as astral projection or out of body experience. Most people have experienced astral travel at one point in their lives. Some of them are aware that they have, while some others are not. You can easily achieve involuntary astral travel when you sleep, or when you're physically exhausted or emotionally stressed. The most obvious sign that your astral body has left your physical body is when you jerk awake when you're in deep sleep, or when you have flying or falling dreams, or when you have a strong sense of déjà vu.

Astral travel is a wonderful experience, and you will want to do it again and again whenever you wish when you get the hang of it. When your astral body leaves your physical body, you can go wherever you like, visit whomever you wish, and explore places that are a great distance away on the physical plane. Some people who have advanced astral traveling experiences have the ability to bend through time and visit the past and the future.

What are the benefits of this type of travel?

Those who practice astral projection report that it is an experience like no other. Astral travelers tell stories of being able to fly around the universe in their adventures. Would you like the experience of being able to visit whomever you please in another realm? Perhaps you'd like to connect with your ancestors of spiritual mentors. Astral travel makes this and a whole lot more possible. Are you ready for your adventure?

Certain crystals have metaphysical properties that support the astral travel process. Crystals are known to store and transmit energy. They help in the cleansing process and when picked up in the palm of the hand they can absorb the negative energy from within the person holding the stone. They are also known to intensify the personal vibrations that are necessary to activate the astral travel experience.

- **Angelite:** This rare stone is milky blue in appearance and it is one of the best stones for aiding any kind of spiritual journey. It is thought to help in making contact with angels and building psychic powers. Once in contact with these spiritual powers in the universe, people report a greater sense of calm and harmony in the earthly world. Angelite is also used for seekers who are trying to find their place in spiritual communities.

- **Moonstone:** Moonstones come in a variety of colors and have a milky appearance. As one might guess, this mineral is named for its qualities that are like the moon. It is known for its feminine qualities and it helps people become more graceful in daily life. Are you having trouble navigating the regular difficulties of life? This may be a stone you might want to try working with during meditation or astral travel.

- **Moldavite:** Moldavite has an olive green color and is thought to be the result of a meteor in Germany. It is unique because it is the only interplanetary mineral known to humankind. Moldavite is said to make the astral travel process go more smoothly by making the exit from the body and the return to the body much more gentle. If you desire more progress in your evolution, try working with Molvite. Like other stones, it helps bring up suppressed memories and issues and helps with the healing process.

- **Malachite:** Malachite is a stunning green stone with bands of variation in color. It is sometimes referred to as the "mirror of the soul." It is not recommended for working with physical illnesses. Malachite is thought to intensify the state one is already in so if you are experiencing a negative state of being it's better to avoid this stone. Malachite is used as a method of protection and as an aid in times of transition.

- **Sapphire:** Sapphire is associated with joy. Used with the throat chakra, it is used to promote lucid dreaming, dream retention and astral travel. It has also been used to relieve anxiety and depression. Sapphire is thought to be particularly useful for doing healing work related to difficult relationships. Are you someone who is looking to widen your sense of awe and beauty in the world? Sapphire is the stone to use for attracting more of this into your life.

- **Azurite:** Known for its azure blue color, azurite possesses strong metaphysical power and it is used for clarity and insight. It balances the mind and reduces emotional instability. Azurite fosters lively engagement with the world because it opens up the mind and spirit to new insights. Using this stone is conducive to meditation and astral travel because it allows one to go deep without fear and trepidation. Azurite releases stress and tension which makes for a more relaxed state that is more likely to be receptive to spiritual endeavors.

- **Quartz:** Quartz is the most commonly cited crystal to use in astral projection. It is used for a variety of healing purposes. Clear quartz crystals are recommended for balancing the energy of any other crystal that is being used. When using quartz, try lying down and placing it on the third eye/sixth chakra for maximum results. If your crystal is small enough, carry it around at all times for extra energy protection.

☐ **Blue Calcite:** This stone is said to produce calm in people who work with it on a regular basis. Blue calcite enhances psychic abilities along with helping to promote astral travel ability. From a health perspective, it can be used to lowering blood pressure and stabilizing the heartbeat. Blue calcite can be found in a variety of colors and people all over the world use it for energetic protection. Feeling a little sluggish? Blue calcite can be used to increase energy and vitality, too.

☐ **Ametrine:** Ametrine is a quartz crystal that combines amethyst and citrine and it said to be an uncommon quartz. When used for astral travel, it's recommended to put it on the solar plexus for best results. Ametrine quartz is used for fending off psychic attacks while traveling in the astral realm. It is also known for helping to bring long buried issues to the surface. Ametrine helps with the following: acceptance of others, mental clarity and releasing blockages.

- ☐ **Vanadinite:** Vanadinite is an uncommon mineral and was first discovered in Mexico. Other names for it are johnstonite and lead vanadate. It is most useful by placing it on the sacral chakra which, in turn, brings energy to all of the lower chakras. It brings a sense of peace and harmony with the universe and it is frequently used with prayer, meditation and astral travel. It is also said to be helpful in warding off sicknesses—even major ones such as cancer.

Using crystals to help facilitate the astral journey is widely believed to be an important piece of preparing the journey. It is worth the investment of time and money in order to achieve the goal of having an astral experience. By using crystals, journeyers purify their energy and attract more positive spirits and experiences while in the astral realm.

CHAPTER TWO

UNLOCK THE SECRETS OF CRYSTAL MEDITATION

Meditation is beneficial to your total well-being by instilling calm and a deep sense of relaxation. It is from this quiet space that creativity is birthed, healing is ignited, and peace is created. Meditation is extremely beneficial for every part of our being—our mind, our body and our spirit. It helps us to relax, clears our mind and releases negative energy and unwanted thoughts. Using crystals for meditation is a powerful tool to deepen your meditation, as well as achieve a specific outcome during your meditation. On a spiritual level, meditating with crystals can help to raise your consciousness and awareness, deepening your intuition and bringing insight.

People visit Energy Muse's store on a daily basis to meditate with different healing stones and crystals to get a feel for their energies. With such a large movement for everyone to incorporate an aspect of meditation into their daily lives, we're constantly asked which are the best crystals for meditation. Any stone or crystal can be used for meditation. Crystals are the tools to help you start and maintain your meditation practice, connect with a specific intention or goal and move into deeper states of meditation. However, the more you begin to practice meditating with crystals, the more you'll want to experience different energies. Use the guidelines below for meditating with crystals.

Ways to Use Crystals for Meditation

Meditate with a Crystal for Your Intention

It is beneficial to choose a crystal that contains healing properties or energies that are in line with what you want to achieve out of your meditation. Setting intentions and meditating with your crystal each morning enhances and magnifies your results. When your mind is focused on your intention from the stillness of your meditation and energy of the crystal, you will have better motivation and inspiration for achieving your goals or receiving certain energy.

Create a Crystal Grid Layout for Meditating with Crystals

Laying stones or crystals on your body allows the healing properties of stones to activate that area of your body. Creating a crystal layout on your body can help you meditate and heal simultaneously.

Choosing a Crystal for Meditation

When it comes time for meditation, how do you choose which crystal to work with? If you are working on something specific in your life, get clear on what that is and perhaps write it down. Choose the crystal that aligns with your goal. (For example, if you are working on bringing in more abundance, citrine may be helpful.) If you are unsure of the significance of a stone, simply do a search on the internet or purchase a book with the descriptions and meanings. Or, you can use your intuition.

When you begin to feel more comfortable using your crystals, practice letting the crystal choose you. You can try this when purchasing a new crystal in a store as well. Close your eyes and ask one of the following questions: "Which crystal is best for me at this time" or "Which crystal can help with a certain problem?" The trick is letting go of doubt and go with the first thought that comes to your mind or notice what attracts your attention. Trust yourself (and the stone)!

How to Meditate with Crystals

After you have chosen your crystal, you are ready for your meditation. There is no right or wrong way to meditate; just as there is no right or wrong crystal to use, everyone's meditations are unique. The best way to utilize your crystals during your meditation is to

1) Hold them in your hands while meditating or

 2) Lay them on your body, ideally so that they touch your skin. If you are new to meditating with crystals, here is a simple daily meditation with crystals to use to help you get started:

- ☐ First, find a quiet space where you feel comfortable and relaxed.
- ☐ Sit quietly with the healing stones or crystals that you wish to use nearby.
- ☐ Close your eyes and quiet your mind, focusing your attention on your breathing
- ☐ Pick up the crystals or stones and hold them comfortably in your hands.
- ☐ Imagine your awareness spiraling down into the stone, feeling the energy of your crystal.
- ☐ Breathe in the highest white light, and let the crystal's energy fill your mind and permeate your senses.
- ☐ Visualize your intention. Your crystals and stones are listening.

- ☐ RELAX your mind and your body. Sit with your crystals as long as you need.

- ☐ When you are finished, and feel completely relaxed and at peace, complete the grounding process by seeing all aspects of your awareness spiraling back out of the crystal and into your body. Feel yourself connect with the Earth and your body.

- ☐ Open your eyes and take a few deep breaths.

CHAPTER THREE

DISCOVER THE FORMATION OF CRYSTAL TYPES

The type of atom and the arrangement of bonds dictate what type of crystal is formed. Knowing this can be useful, as a crystal's formation may enhance its action. The process of forming a crystal is called crystallization. Crystallization commonly occurs when a solid crystal grows from a liquid or solution. As a hot solution cools or a saturated solution evaporates, particles draw close enough for chemical bonds to form. Crystals can also form from deposition directly from the gas phase. Liquid crystals possess particles oriented in an organized manner, like solid crystals, yet able to flow.

Crystals Grouped by Lattices (Shape)

There are seven crystal lattice systems.

1. **Cubic or Isometric:** These are not always cube-shaped. You'll also find octahedrons (eight faces) and dodecahedrons (10 faces). The cubic crystal structure has the loveliest and good symmetry. All angels are equal to

90° with equal length measurement on all sides.

2. **Tetragonal:** Similar to cubic crystals, but longer along one axis than the other, these crystals forming double pyramids and prisms.

3. **Orthorhombic:** Like tetragonal crystals except not square in cross-section (when viewing the crystal on end), these crystals form rhombic prisms or dipyramids (two pyramids stuck together).

4. **Hexagonal:** When you look at the crystal on end, the cross-section is a six-sided prism or hexagon.

5. **Trigonal:** These crystals possess a single 3-fold axis of rotation instead of the 6-fold axis of the hexagonal division.

6. **Triclinic:** These crystals are not usually symmetrical from one side to the other, which can lead to some fairly strange shapes.

7. **Monoclinic:** Like skewed tetragonal crystals, these crystals often form prisms and double pyramids.

This is a very simplified view of crystal structures. In addition, the lattices can be primitive (only one lattice point per unit cell) or non-primitive (more than one lattice point per unit cell). Combining the 7 crystal systems with the 2 lattice types yields the 14 Bravais Lattices (named after Auguste Bravais, who worked out lattice structures in 1850).

Crystals Grouped by Properties

There are four main categories of crystals, as grouped by their chemical and physical properties.

1. **Covalent Crystals:** A covalent crystal has true covalent bonds between all of the atoms in the crystal. You can think of a covalent crystal as one big molecule. Many covalent crystals have extremely high melting points. Examples of covalent crystals include diamond and zinc sulfide crystals.

2. **Metallic Crystals:** Individual metal atoms of metallic crystals sit on lattice sites. This leaves the outer electrons of these atoms free to float around the lattice. Metallic crystals tend to be very dense and have high melting points.

3. **Ionic Crystals:** The atoms of ionic crystals are held together by electrostatic forces (ionic bonds). Ionic crystals are hard and have relatively high melting points. Table salt (NaCl) is an example of this type of crystal.

4. **Molecular Crystals:** These crystals contain recognizable molecules within their structures. A molecular crystal is held together by non-covalent interactions, like van der Waals forces or hydrogen bonding. Molecular crystals tend to be soft with relatively low melting points. Rock candy, the crystalline form of table sugar or sucrose, is an example of a molecular crystal.

As with the lattice classification system, this system isn't completely cut-and-dried. Sometimes it's hard to categorize crystals as belonging to one class as opposed to another. However, these broad groupings will provide you with some understanding of structures.

CHAPTER FOUR

APPLY THE ART OF CRYSTAL CLEANSING

Cleansing

The lure of beautiful crystals cannot be denied. Whether you have 1 or 100, they speak to us in ways that we know we must bring them home. I see our role as guardian rather than owner, for their gifts to us are massive, but they like to be co-creators rather than indentured servants to humanity. When you get a crystal, it may be new to you, but it's been on a long journey to reach its final destination in the palms of your hands. It's been plucked from a mine, passed off to different handlers, who then gave it to a vendor, to sell to a retailer, where it got touched by various customers before it was selected by you! That's a lot of collected energy you don't want to work with. Because we all want a fresh start for our new journey with our crystals, it's crucial that the first step you take is cleansing your crystals.

Luckily, there are lots of ways for cleansing your crystals, and many of them can be as therapeutic to your own spirit as they are for your stones. From getting some rest and relaxation by the light of moon, or enjoying a nice sound bath, these are some fun methods for cleansing your crystals to get both you and your crystal in the highest, purified spirits.

Use them as often as needed. Your crystal's energy can get overloaded and dull, just like your own. So be sure to do a periodic crystal cleansing to get the most out of your continued work with your stone.

Why is cleansing important?

Many people use crystals to soothe their mind, body, and soul. Some believe that crystals act on an energetic level, sending natural vibrations out into the world. Crystals often travel long distances, from source to seller, before a purchase is made. Each transition exposes the stone to energies that may be misaligned with your own. And when used for healing, these stones are said to absorb or redirect the negativity you're working to release. Regularly cleansing and recharging your stones is the only way to restore your crystal to its natural state. This act of care can also reinvigorate your own sense of purpose.

How to Program Your Crystal

In the same way that you need a sense of direction in order to be the best you can be, so does your crystal. Crystals want to work for you, but you need to give them a job. Crystals are neutral; they don't judge situations as good or bad. They are also amplifiers, and when they are not programmed, can amplify things in your life that you don't want – because they need to channel their energy in a specific direction. Giving your crystal a job allows you to set your intention for the work you'll do together. It creates a certain synergy between you and your crystal ally. Get specific! For the crystal to help you bring your transformation to light, you have to be clear when programming your crystal.

1. First, cleanse your crystal.
2. Hold it in your hands, close your eyes and take three deep breaths in through the nose and out through the mouth.
3. Reflect on your faith, the Earth and what makes you happy. This will connect you with your highest vibration.

4. While in this space of love and light, ask that your crystal be cleared of all unwanted energy and any previous programming. Aloud or in your head, say: I ask that the highest vibration of love and light connect with my highest self to clear all unwanted energy and any previous programming. I command this crystal to hold the intention of... To finish this sentence, add three intentions for your crystal – energies you wish it to hold for you.

5. End your programming by saying thank you three times. By saying it three times, you emphasize that what you're asking for already exists in the universe.

Methods to cleanse, charge and program crystals

Be Clear in Mind

The purpose of cleaning is to bring the crystal to a clear and pure state. Crystals are frozen vibrations after all and any impurities and discord it experiences during its harvest, sale and journey will be felt. As you are working with purification, being of clear mind and intention is necessary. Say a mantra, clear the room with sage or bells and be ready to let the purest light move from you. The cleansing is a ritual after all and all such endeavors require mindful peace and vigilance.

A Crystallized Cleansing with Quartz or Selenite

Be a crystal matchmaker and pair your crystal with either a selenite or quartz crystal! Both of these crystals have the unique ability to cleanse, recharge and purify the energy of other crystals, without diminishing their own energy. Lay your crystals and tumbled stones on a piece of Clear quartz or a selenite charging plate for 6+ hours. We like to make it a practice with the jewelry and crystals that we use daily to place them atop these cleansing crystals before bed each night. Then, when you wake in the morning, they will be ready to work with you.

When in Doubt, Smoke It Out

Not only will burning Sage and Frankincense, and Palo Santo make your home smell great, they'll have your crystals feeling great, too. Immerse your crystals in the sacred smoke until it seems to come back to life. This is likely the best option for larger, harder to pick up crystals. Simply use your feather or your hand to waft the smoke over and around the crystal.

Water

Water is a master energy and can be used in any form of ritual. With crystals and water, their legacy is entwined and they are amicable partners for assisting each other.

1. You may hold the crystal under water (pure spring or a river/ocean is most ideal, but we make due!)
2. Visualize the water washing over the crystal taking away any disruptions to its natural state

3. Use sea salt and lightly brush it over the stone using the water to cleanse the salt away

*Note not all crystals can withstand water. Some, like selenite, will dissolve. Please do your homework before immersing your beloved under water.

Return to Nature

We could all use an energetic reset in nature every now and then. To give your crystal that revitalizing pleasure, place it on the soil or even bury it within the Earth for 24 hours. If you have a clean stream, creek or body of water nearby, submerge your crystal in the running water for a few moments, making sure to do so with the intention to purify in mind.

Note: make sure you are mindful when placing certain crystals in water; many of the softer ones that are salt-based will dissolve when they get wet.

Snow

Not everyone is fortunate enough to share this special blessing, but placing your cherished crystals in snow is a quick and powerful way to clear and program your crystals to hold long lasting intent.

Sunlight or Moonlight Spa

When you see your crystals starting to look a little dull and not as vibrant, return them to nature. Let your crystals bathe outside in light of the sun or moon for at least 4 hours. Especially with the large crystals in your home, although it can be a process, make sure that you place them outside to clear and recharge at least once a month.

Sound

Long trusted by the ancients, a bell is an easy ally to remind you how to take care of your crystals. Likewise the sound of your own voice and the use of sacred chants will hold the programming.

When to Clear

Besides when first acquiring, a crystal will absorb energy as it "works." Each has its own purpose and like people, needs a rest, a recharge, from time to time. You may notice your crystal feeling heavy or dull or you may intuitively get a message that it needs some refreshing. Any particularly intense work – after a fight or during times of illness or trauma, for instance – crystals can best serve you if they are cleared before being put back to work.

CHAPTER FIVE

LEARN THE TRUTH ABOUT

CHAKRAS AND CRYSTAL SCIENCE

Chakra is an old Sanskrit word that literally translates to wheel. This is because the life force, or prana, that moves inside of you is spinning and rotating. This spinning energy has 7 centers in your body, starting at the base of your spine and moving all the way up to the top of your head. In a healthy, balanced person, the 7 chakras provide exactly the right amount of energy to every part of your body, mind and spirit. However, if one of your chakras is too open and spinning too quickly, or if it is too closed and moving slowly, your health will suffer.

By learning about the 7 chakras, you can become more in tune with the natural energy cycles of your body. You can use this information to connect physical, emotional and spiritual imbalances with the chakras that empower them. Of course, with those discoveries you can begin to balance your chakras and live a healthy and harmonious life.

The 7 chakras for beginners

Before diving right into learning about the **seven chakras** and what each of them do, take a moment now to tune in to your body and see if you can feel your chakras at work. For beginners, those chakra exercises may seem "odd" – simply go with the flow and soon, you will not be a chakra beginner any longer. You may sense the prana energy centers very lightly, very intensely or not at all. Whatever happens is ok. Think of this exercise like an introduction; you're tuning in for, perhaps, the very first time.

☐ First, start by making sure you're in a quiet space. If you can't be right now, just return to this section of the article later. But if you can, sit quietly for a moment and take a few deep breaths. Let tension and stress slide away for just a moment. Just be in the moment, with your body.

☐ Now, bring your attention to the base of your spine, your tailbone, and imagine a bright spinning red light. Feel it pulsing and rotating with your breath. Sit with that for a moment.

- ☐ Move your attention up your spine to the area a couple of inches below your belly button. Feel the warmth of a bright, orange spinning light. Again, notice how it moves with your breath.

- ☐ Guide your attention further up to a couple inches above your belly button. You're probably familiar with this area, because when you feel strong emotions like love or fear, you likely feel it here. Notice how you can sense the intense yellow light rotating in that spot.

- ☐ Bring your attention further up to the center of your chest where your heart is. This area harnesses a bright green light. When you're touched or moved, you might instinctively place your hand over this spot. Connect with that area now.

☐ Then, bring your attention to your throat, the dip in between your collar bones. Imagine a bright blue light spinning in that area. You may feel the urge to swallow or clear your throat as you think of it.

☐ Next, move your attention up to the space on your forehead between your eyebrows, your third eye. This area holds a deep indigo rotating light. Imagine yourself becoming wiser as it spins and becomes brighter.

☐ Finally, shift your attention to the very top of your head. Imagine a vibrant, spinning violet light that shines right out of the top of your body. This light connects you to the universe. Feel the peace that comes with noticing this light.

☐ Wear T-shirt featuring Seven Chakras to strengthen and balance your chakras.

The Seven Chakras: Meaning and Symbols

Now that you've been introduced to your chakras, let's talk about the role that each of them plays in your life. I am going to discuss the location and purpose of each chakra, and i will also talk about the symptoms you might experience when they are balanced or imbalanced. Of course, each discussion will conclude with how to heal, empower or tame each chakra.

1. The Root Chakra
2. The Sacral Chakra
3. The Solar Plexus Chakra
4. The Heart Chakra
5. The Throat Chakra
6. The 3rd Eye Chakra
7. The Crown Chakra

The 1st Chakra – Root Chakra – Muladhara

The official name of this chakra, muladhara, comes from the words Mula, which means root and Dhara, which means support. So, this chakra's role is to connect all of your energy with the Earth, which is called grounding. When you think of your Root Chakra, think of your day to day survival here on earth. This energy center's role is to give you everything you need to survive. For us in this modern age, that typically translates to financial and emotional security.

Color: Red

Location: This chakra is located at the very base of your spine, near your tailbone. It goes up to just below your belly button.

What balanced feels like: When your 1st chakra is balanced, you will feel a sense of accomplishment and peace when you think about things like money, safety and shelter.

You will feel connected to your human experience.

When this chakra is overactive: Our root chakra gets a lot of use, so having an overactive one is very common.

When is your 1st chakra overactive

An overactive root chakra will cause problems like anxiety and jitteriness. This happens because fear is based out of the need to survive. That is fear's role – to keep us alive. So, an overactive root chakra will shout messages of survival, even when no real threat is there; thus, you will have anxiety problems. Physically, you might have symptoms of digestive problems, lower back issues, hip pain, ovarian cysts in women or prostate issues in men.

How to balance your 1st chakra

In practical terms, it's important to take care of your survival needs first. This chakra gives you the energy to do that, so utilize that energy to the best of your ability.

Then, calm this chakra by focusing on your connection to spirit. Take time each day to nurture your soul by praying, meditating or connecting to spirit guides.

Volunteering and acts of kindness and compassion can guide overactive energy away from your root chakra and into other energy centers in your body.

When is the 1st chakra underactive

If your survival needs have generally been taken care of, this chakra may not have been very active throughout your life.

If that's the case, you may experience frequent day dreaming, trouble concentrating or simply feeling like your "head's in the clouds." People may say you appear "airheaded" or "spacey." These may not seem like major issues, but being balanced and connected is important.

Energize your 1st chakra

If you find yourself disconnected from material existence, your 1st chakra may need to be revved up. You can do this with reconnecting to the earth by being out in nature. Gardening, swimming or even playing in the leaves can energize your root chakra. You can also get yourself a t-shirt featuring Muladhara to strengthen your Root Chakra.

The 2nd chakra – Sacral Chakra – Svadhishana

The 2nd chakra is the sacral chakra or svadhishana which translates to "the place of the self." This chakra is all about your identity as a human and what you do with it. Your sacral chakra is the home of the creative life force energy that helps you enjoy your life here on Earth. It's the energy that motivates you to enjoy the fruits of your labor including indulging in pleasurable activities like sex.

Color: Orange

Location: The sacral chakra is located right below the belly button and extends to its center.

What balanced feels like: When your 2nd chakra is balanced, you will relish in the pleasurable things life has to offer, without overdoing them.

Sex, good food and creative activities will be inspiring and enjoyable, and you will get a sense of wellness and abundance from them.

When this chakra is overactive

The sacral chakra is often overactive when we face things like addiction and gluttony. Pleasure is a good thing, and you should never feel guilty for enjoying the good things life has to offer. However, if you find yourself enjoying things that aren't nourishing for your soul or healthy for you, then your sacral chakra is likely out of balance. Symptoms include addiction, obesity, hormone imbalances and restlessness.

How to balance your 2nd chakra

To balance your 2nd chakra, it's helpful to draw energy away from pleasure and into your heart.

You can do this by asking yourself a simple question before each action you take. Ask yourself, "Is what I am about to do good for me? Is it healthy and nourishing? What are the benefits of the action I'm about to take? "

Taking time to assess whether your actions are healthy is a great way to draw energy away from this chakra.

When this chakra is underactive

If you've spent a lot of time focusing on very practical things without enjoying the fruits of your labor, your sacral chakra may be underactive. Symptoms of this include depression, impotence, decreased sex drive and a lack of passion and creativity.

How to energize your 2nd chakra

Energizing your 2nd chakra is fun. In simple terms – enjoy life! Create a piece of art. Eat a healthy and enjoyable snack. Make love to your partner.

Take time for yourself and enjoy the incredible gifts the Earth has to offer you.

The 3rd chakra – Solar Plexus – Manipura

The 3rd chakra is the Solar Plexus or Manipura which translates to "lustrous gem." This chakra is where your self-confidence, identity and personal power are born. Have you ever been in a situation that you just knew wasn't right for you?

Perhaps you've been in a situation that you knew was going to work out. Where did you feel those cues in your body. Most people say they feel those types of cues in their "gut." In reality, this is the seat of your personal power, your solar plexus, and you can physically feel that confidence and wisdom in its location.

Color: Yellow

Location: The solar plexus starts in the center of the belly button and extends up to the breastbone or where your two sets of ribs connect in the center of your chest.

What balanced feels like: When your 3rd chakra is balanced, you will feel a sense of wisdom, decisiveness and personal power.

Many call this chakra the warrior chakra, as the feeling you get from it is comparable to a wise warrior going into battle.

He has the confidence to win and the wisdom to know the personal truth he is fighting for.

When this chakra is overactive

The solar plexus chakra becomes overactive when the power we have over our own lives extends into the lives of others. When this chakra is too energized, you may feel quick to anger, the need to control and micromanage, greediness and a lack of compassion or empathy. You may suffer from digestive issues or even imbalances in your internal organs like the appendix, pancreas, liver and kidneys.

How to balance your 3rd chakra

To balance your 3rd chakra, practice opening up your heart with love and compassion. Meditate on sending love and kindness from your heart to all those around you. Refocus the power you have and see yourself as a beacon of love.

When this chakra is underactive

When our personal power is taken away from us either by another person or through extenuating circumstances, we may be left with a lack of energy in our 3rd chakra. When this happens, you may feel indecisive, insecure, timid and needy.

How to energize your 3rd chakra

To energize your Solar Plexus, think of the things that you know you're good at. Everyone has talents and abilities. Make a list of yours. Feel how the confidence in those talents makes your stomach tingle and vibrate. Empower that feeling by creating your own personal affirmations.

The 4th chakra – Heart – Anahata

The 4th chakra is the Heart or Anahata chakra, which translates to "unhurt." This chakra is where your love, compassion and kindness are empowered. It's not hard to understand this chakra. We all associate our hearts with love, and that's exactly what the 4th chakra is all about. This includes love for others and love for yourself, which is why this chakra is also associated with health and healing.

Color: Green

Location: The heart chakra's center is located right over your heart and it radiates down to your breastbone and up to your throat.

What balanced feels like: When your 4th chakra is balanced, you are able to equally feel love for yourself and others. Even when tough things happen, you can still see the compassion and kindness in others.

When this chakra is overactive

When the heart chakra becomes overactive, we lose our personal boundaries and start to make unhealthy choices, all in the name of love. It's important to treat yourself with the same compassion and kindness that you give others, but when the heart chakra is overactive, you may find yourself always putting the needs of others before your own. Symptoms include a fast heart rate, palpitations, heart burn and interpersonal relationship issues.

How to balance your 4th chakra

Balancing your 4th chakra means taking that love you've given to others and focusing some of it back on yourself. You can do this by doing 1 thing every day that's just for you:

- ☐ Take a relaxing bath
- ☐ Treat yourself to a massage
- ☐ Meditate on sending compassion to yourself

When this chakra is underactive

Many people have an underactive 4th chakra. Life can send us a lot of heartbreak as a way to teach us lessons about ourselves and the world around us. But, it can be hard to not take those lessons personally. When your heart chakra is underactive, you will feel like it's hard to get really close to anyone. It's like building a wall around your heart and not letting anyone in. Physically, you may feel out of touch with your body and suffer from circulation problems.

How to energize your 4th chakra

Energizing your heart chakra may take a lot of work. Many of us have worked hard to build up our walls and defenses, and it isn't always easy to knock them down. It first begins by loving yourself. Show appreciation for yourself, and give yourself the love that you want others to give to you. Then, spread that compassion to those around you.

The 5th Chakra – Throat – Vishuddha

The 5th chakra is the Throat chakra or Vishuddha which translates to "very pure." This chakra gives a voice to your personal truths. Where does your voice come from? What provides the energy for you to speak?

On a physical level, of course the answer is the throat, but on an energetic level, this energy actually comes from your 5th chakra. This chakra lets you speak your truth with clarity. Resting right above the heart, the throat chakra is connected to the compassion and love you have for yourself and others.

Color: Blue

Location: The throat chakra's center is right in between your collar bone, and it radiates down to the center of your heart and up to the center of your eyes.

What balanced feels like: When your throat chakra is balanced, you will be able to clearly speak with love, kindness and truth.

You will know exactly which words are appropriate for each situation. Speaking with a balanced throat chakra will enlighten and inspire those around you.

When this chakra is overactive

Our 5th chakra becomes overactive when we've spent a lot of time trying to make our voice heard.

If you've often felt ignored or invalidated when you express yourself, you may have tried to overcome this by giving yourself a louder voice.

Those with overactive throat chakras will often interrupt others, often be told they have a loud voice or "love to hear themselves talk." Physically, you may suffer from throat pain, frequent infections, cavities or mouth ulcers.

How to balance your 5th chakra

Balancing your 5th chakra is as easy as thinking before you speak.

Take it from the Buddha, before you say anything, ask yourself.

When this chakra is underactive

Sometimes, we have been ignored and invalidated so much that we react in an opposite way – we shut down our voices and never speak our truth. If you have an underactive throat chakra, you have likely been called shy or quiet. You may find yourself unable to express your emotions or struggling for words when you try to speak your truth. Physical symptoms often include digestive issues, because energy diverted away from the throat chakra often ends up being "swallowed" or sent down to the 3rd chakra.

How to energize your 5th chakra

Speak your truth!

Even if no one is around to hear you, practice expressing your emotions and truths when you're alone.

It's very common to think that we should only speak when someone else is around to hear it, but if you're trying to energize your fifth chakra, it doesn't matter if its received by any other ear than your own.

The 6th Chakra – The Third Eye – Ajna

The 6th chakra is the Third Eye Chakra Ajna which translates to "beyond wisdom." This chakra opens up your mind to information beyond the material world and the 5 senses. Extra sensory perception, intuition or psychic energy, all comes from the third eye. There is actually a small pinecone shaped gland in your brain that takes in light. This gland, the pineal gland, is responsible for helping you feel awake in the daytime and sleepy at night. Long before brain imaging, ancient cultures knew this Third Eye existed, and they also realized that it receives information from sources outside of the five senses.

Color: Indigo

Location: The third eye's center is in between your eyebrows. It radiates down to your mouth and up to the top of your head.

What balanced feels like: A balanced third eye is a beautiful thing, and it's really what you are trying to achieve when you start on a path to spiritual development.

When your third eye chakra is balanced, you will equally feel in tune with both the physical world and the material world. You will receive psychic information as frequently as you receive information from your 5 physical senses, but it will not overwhelm you.

When this chakra is overactive

It is very unlikely your 6th chakra is overactive. Most of us are very in tune with our physical reality and find it difficult to receive information outside of it. That being said, if you have an overactive third eye, you likely spend most of your time engrossed in psychic activities like tarot card readings, astrology and paranormal experiences. When your 3rd eye chakra is overactive, those activities become overwhelming and distract you from living a human experience.

How to balance your 6th chakra

If you find yourself consumed with psychic information, take some time to remind yourself that you are a creature of the Earth.

Go to the beach and feel the sand on your toes. Dig your in the dirt in your garden. Connect your body to Earth and repeat:

When this chakra is underactive

Most people have an underactive 6th chakra. We live in a world that often invalidates intuitive development. Because of this, we close off our Third Eyes and ignore our own psychic experiences. Doing so can cause us to feel disconnected from spiritual experiences. Physically, you may feel headaches or have problems with allergies and your sinuses.

How to energize your 6th chakra

Energizing your third eye will take some practice. You'll need to devote some time to quiet, solitary meditation. At first, get used to the feeling of focusing on signals outside of your physical body. Listen to your spirit and recognize how that feels. As you practice this, you'll find it easier and easier to connect with the energy from your Third Eye.

The 7th Chakra – Crown – Sahaswara

The 7th chakra is the Crown or Sahaswara, which translates to "thousand petaled." This chakra is pure consciousness energy. The Crown chakra is one of those energies that's hard to explain. You can think of it like magnetism. When you hold a piece of metal to a magnet, you can feel the energy and tension, but you can't see it. Consciousness energy is everywhere and in everything. It connects us to the entire universe.

Our own personal consciousness is located in the 7th chakra, but it's really more like the seed of a universal energy than something personal or individual.

Color: Violet – White

Location: The crown chakra's center is at the top of your head. It radiates down to between your eyes and then extends infinitely upward and outward, connecting you to the energy of the rest of the universe.

What balanced feels like: Achieving a balanced crown chakra is the goal of every spiritual warrior, and it's not easy to do. You can think of it like the Buddhist concept of achieving nirvana.

Once you achieve it, you're not really human anymore – you've conquered suffering and death. Of course, it is the journey of attempting to achieve this balance that brings us happiness, good health and wisdom. Trying to balance your 7th chakra will align and balance your other chakras.

When this chakra is overactive

It's not possible to have an overactive crown chakra.

Because it is the seat of universal energy, it is innately infinite. In other words, you can't exist in the material world and be overcome with consciousness energy.

How to balance your 7th chakra

Since no one has an overactive crown chakra, there's no need to consider how to calm the energy down.

When this chakra is underactive

An underactive 7th chakra means you're human.

It feels exactly like being a human. Some people may be closer to achieving it, while others may be far away. In any case, practicing spiritual development and balancing your other chakras will bring your closer to experiencing the consciousness energy in your crown chakra.

How to energize your 7th chakra

Instead of attempting to open up and active your crown chakra, focus on balancing the other 6 chakras.

Meditate and connect with spirit and balance those activities with living and enjoying your human experience.

Think of it like trying to win an Olympic gold medal. You don't just try to win the medal, you train your body and mind first. The only way to achieve such a huge goal is to focus on small, attainable goals first.

The same goes for trying to open your crown chakra. Don't just attempt it; focus on maintaining and balancing all the other energies in your body.

WHAT CRYSTALS AFFECT CHAKRAS BEST

Every stone has a unique vibration, just as every person does. For this reason, the particular stones needed for balancing the chakras will vary somewhat from person to person. For this reason, you see a lot of different suggestions across various chakra books. The best way to determine if a particular gemstone is good for you or for a specific chakra is to "test" it by placing it on your body and checking in with your body's subtle (or sometimes, not-so-subtle) response. You may even want to have a friend place different stones on your body while your eyes are closed, and determine which ones feel the best on each chakra.

Always trust your body's response. If a stone feels bad on the body, remove it – unless you recognize that "bad" feeling as a clearing, and feel an instinctive desire to stay with the stone. A very simple, but generally good rule for chakra balancing is that if a stone is the color of the chakra, it's good for boosting and balancing that chakra. Hence, the first chakra stones tend to be red-toned, the second chakra stones orange-toned, and so on. Certain stones, like quartz, come in many different hues and can be used for all of the chakras depending on its shade.

When picking which gemstones to use for each chakra, secondary colors should be considered. Two common ones are: black for the root chakra and pink for the heart chakra.This does not mean that every stone that heals a particular chakra will be the primary or secondary color of that chakra. There are exceptions. Still, there is so much correspondence between the gemstones' color and the chakras they balance, that it is a great "rule of thumb" – especially for anyone who doesn't know a lot about rocks.

CRYSTAL USES IN SCIENCE AND TECHNOLOGY

The most notable and the most popular out of all the types of crystal that exist is clear quartz, also known as rock crystal. Quartz is known as the "master healer", due to its alleged capacity to help heal many ailments. It is also believed to be able to retain and store huge amounts of information for future usage.

Quartz Crystals Enable Data Storage

If you're already skeptical about the alleged power of quartz crystal, there are a few things you may want to consider, for example, how many of you have a laptop, computer monitor or mobile phone which uses an LCD display?

LCD, of course, stands for liquid crystal display. That's right, crystals are used in the screens of many electronic devices. Although LED (light emitting diode) screens are now becoming more popular, until recently, LCD screens had become the standard model . . . and that's just the tip of the iceberg. One of the most credible facts supporting the alleged power of quartz crystal, is the way that microchips work. Of course, microchips are used in all sorts of modern technologies, from mobile phones and computers, to rockets and missiles. It was the microchip that revolutionized the world of technology, brought us modern computing and also revolutionized space travel.

You may want to ask yourself, how is it that microchips can continue to store data even when there is no electronic power being fed to your device? For example, you can turn your computer off and take the battery out, but even when you start it back up again, the computer still knows what to do—the information it needs to function is retained within the microchips, even when there is no power source. It was also announced fairly recently that quartz has the ability to store data for up to three million years! How?

The answer to this lies in silica dioxide.

Silica Dioxide Is a Naturally Occurring Element Used in Electronics

Silica dioxide or quartz has been known about for thousands of years. It is a constituent of sand and is most often found in nature in the form of quartz. Amazingly, quartz is also found in many living biological organisms.

Silica dioxide is an important component for the functionality of computers and other similar electronic devices. In other words, if quartz crystal didn't have the attributed value of being able to store large amounts of data, then you wouldn't have the technology to be able to read this book. It's the storage capacity of the quartz crystal contained within your device (computer) that makes it possible for you to be able to view this book in the first place. Without the storage capacity of quartz, you would not be able to do it, and there would be no such thing as computing or other such examples of modern technology. In this respect, you may want to consider how it's allegedly possible to store information within quartz crystal using intent, and how this function is also similarly carried out by computer technology in order to store data . . . and it certainly doesn't end there. In addition, quartz crystals do have technological applications that are related, in a sense, to transforming energy. In technical terms, quartz is piezoelectric, meaning it can transform energy from one form to another.

If any mechanical pressure is applied to a quartz crystal, a voltage will appear across it, which means it can convert mechanical forces into electrical signals. This made it useful in things such as microphones and phonograph needles in earlier days, though now there are better materials for these applications - and, of course, few people still listen to records. Alternatively, if you put voltage across a quartz crystal, it will change shape a little. In other words, it can convert electrical signals into mechanical forces. The effect is small, but is useful, especially in making quartz oscillators. The idea is that you can think of a bit of quartz as a sort of tuning fork that vibrates when struck. That vibration will eventually die out, but if you take the voltage the quartz crystal makes and amplify it (this will cost you some energy from a battery, say), you can then take that voltage and feed it back to the crystal to change its shape at the right moments to keep it vibrating indefinitely. Such an oscillator can be very stable and is the basis for all sorts of electronic devices that require precise standards of timing. Quartz also finds applications in optics because of its high strength and melting point, compared with glass, and its transparency to a much wider range of ultraviolet light.

CHAPTER SIX

ACCESS CELESTIAL ENERGIES BY CHARGING CRYSTALS

A great way to both cleanse and charge your stones is by placing them under the moonlight of a Full Moon. Start by clearing with sage or running them briefly under running water with the intention of cleansing any heavy energy or energy that is not yours. If you are able to place your stones in a safe location outdoors, bring them out and lay them under the light of the Full Moon for a complete Moon Bath. This allows them to charge with the light of the Moon, amplifying their energy and metaphysical healing properties. Depending on the stone, you may also leave outside the next day, for a full cycle charge, Full Moon and Sun, to have the Yin/Yang, Solar/Lunar energy charge to your crystals.

- One of the best times to cleanse and charge crystals, is on the New Moon and Full Moon of every month. Moonlight and Sunlight at any time will cleanse and charge your crystals; however during the New Moon and Full Moon cycles, the moon and planetary energy is much more intense and amplified. This makes the cleanse very powerful.

- ☐ Sunlight is an excellent way to take a dull, overloaded stone and make the energy vibrant again. Sun bathing is a convenient and easy way to cleanse as sunlight is easily accessible. Giving your crystal a sun bath will rid the crystal of excess residual energy and toxicity as well as charge the crystal so it is renewed, revitalized, and ready for use. Sunlight is great for cleansing and charging, however long exposure in the sun can begin to fade your crystals coloring. So it is best to be mindful of how long and how often you sunbathe your crystals when using this method.

- ☐ Moonlight is a great way to cleanse crystals and stones and it is one of my personal favorite methods to use. Moonlight is a natural deep cleanser and is easily accessible to cleanse and charge your stones. As mentioned above, the energy is the most powerful during the new moon and full moon cycles so that is one of the best times to use this method.

☐ Leave your crystals outside to bathe in the moon for at least 4 hours or overnight to achieve a deep cleansing and charging. All of the residual energy, negative energy, and toxicity the crystal has accumulated since your last cleansing will be released and purified so your crystal will be ready to work with its full potential.

☐ If you are concerned with leaving crystals outdoors you can place crystals inside by a window or inside a car by the windshield so they can bathe in the moon or sun without the fear of getting the crystals wet, lost, or damaged by weather.

ASTROLOGY

what is astrology?

For centuries, humans have looked to the heavens for guidance. Astrology is, put simply, the study of the correlation between the astronomical positions of the planets and events on earth. Astrologers believe that the positions of the Sun, Moon, and planets at the time of a person's birth have a direct influence on that person's character. These positions are thought to affect a person's destiny, although many Astrologers feel that free will plays a large role in any individual's life. Astrology can be used as a powerful and fun tool for understanding ourselves, others, and the world around us. We use many different tools, or languages, to define and understand our world. For example, we can use psychological tools and terminology to explore human behavior. Similarly, Astrology gives us rich tools for understanding human character, and offers us a language for communicating our observations with others.

While we can use the natal chart (also called a birth chart or horoscope) as a "window" into any individual or event, we should never use it to pass judgment or to label people. Neither should we use it as an excuse for our behavior! We can never purport to know absolutely everything about someone just because we have their natal chart before us. It is a good idea to approach Astrology as an imperfect language. Even if it were perfect, we are not, so our interpretations can never be considered anywhere close to perfect. It follows to be wary of anyone claiming to be an Astrologer who also alleges to "know all", or makes dire predictions. This kind of practice is not only irresponsible and misleading, it can affect the lives of those who believe them in adverse ways.

Fortunately, obtaining your natal chart is now as simple as gathering your birth information and pointing your browser to a site with a good Astrological chart generating software program. Once you have your chart in hand (or onscreen!), you can learn to interpret it by first learning what the symbols mean.

What's Your Sign?

When a person asks your "sign", even if they don't know it, they are referring to your Sun Sign, which is the zodiacal sign position of the Sun at the time of your birth. Sun Sign Astrology gets a lot of press. However, with a little thought, it is rather intuitive to feel that dividing the entire human population into only 12 categories (the 12 Sun Signs) is far too simplistic. The truth is, every individual on this planet is complex.

While the sign position of the Sun is meaningful, there is much more to Astrology than just the Sun. In fact, Astrology is just as delightfully (and sometimes maddeningly!) complex as people themselves. Besides the sign of the Sun, each person has a Moon sign, Mercury sign, Venus sign, Mars sign, and so forth. Furthermore, each of the planets and luminaries fall in particular houses (there are 12 in all) in their birth charts (also called natal charts). Character is also believed to be influenced by the relationships the planets, luminaries, and points have with each other. Astrologers measure these relationships by the number of degrees between them to determine whether they form an aspect or not.

Countless other refinements can be studied, and this is simply natal chart analysis. Astrologers can turn to a variety of other systems, such as predictive Astrology techniques, Synastry (the study of relationships), and more. The study of Astrology is complex, indeed. You can truly spend a lifetime studying the subject! Fortunately, learning Astrology can be a fun and rewarding endeavor, especially for those with a strong interest in learning more about themselves, others, and their lives. Beginning students of Astrology can take the learning process one step at a time, perhaps starting with the Sun Signs, moving on to a study of the Moon, and so forth. The wonderful reward for this step-by-step approach is the gradual unfolding of your own chart and the charts of those you love!

Is Astrology a Science?

Astrology is best categorized as a metaphysical discipline. It uses a combination of scientific knowledge about the cosmos, scientific tools, intuition, and psychology. It focuses on energy patterns, with a basis in the elements, similar to the studies of yoga, feng shui, numerology, crystal healing, and acupuncture.

How Does Astrology Determine my Horoscope?

A birth chart (or natal chart) is a horoscope (or astrological chart) showing the relative position of planets, angles, points, other heavenly bodies, and the zodiac signs, at the exact moment of birth. The birth chart is calculated using the date, exact time, and place of birth.

How Does Astrology Influence My Personality?

Astrology reflects your personality, along with so many other aspects. Your birth chart is like a map of your Soul, and it can illuminate many things about you. As with any map, it cannot serve as a substitute for a trip to the actual land. You are the most important part of your chart – your level of consciousness, how you are working with your energy, how you choose to experience your circumstances.

The zodiac sign the sun was in the moment you were born (your sun sign) reflects your sense of purpose and how you are meant to shine in the world. Your moon sign reflects your emotional nature, your instinctual nature/reactions, and your mystery. Your rising sign, or ascendant, is the zodiac sign that was rising on the eastern horizon at the moment you were born. Your rising sign reflects how you spontaneously move through life – how you show up in the moment.

There is no single unified theory or practice of astrology. Ancient cultures all practiced their own forms, some of which combined and evolved into today's common western astrology. Eastern cultures continue to practice their own forms of astrology: Chinese, Vedic and Tibetan astrology are among the most well-known. Even within western astrology, there is a considerable diversity of methods and philosophies. Some divide astrology by the end result that is intended:

- **Mundane Astrology** - This is used to examine world events and make predictions about national affairs, wars and economies.

- **Interrogatory Astrology** - This branch can be further subdivided, but generally refers to astrology that seeks to make specific predictions or analyses about the subject's objectives or events within the subject's life.

- **Natal Astrology** - This is what most people think of when they think of astrology. Natal Astrology seeks to make predictions and analyses based on the date of a person's birth. It's based on the idea that everything that happens to something is expressed at the very beginning of that thing, sometimes known as the Law of Beginnings

CHAPTER SEVEN

COMBINE ENERGIES TO MANIFEST CRYSTAL GRIDS

A crystal grid is a crystal arrangement following a specific geometric shape that will focus the Universal Life Force of the crystals in a specific way and for a specific purpose. It is a pattern, created using multiple crystals, that is designed to amplify your intention. The crystals used in the grid are not random but are carefully chosen to create a harmonic relationship between the energies, shapes and colors of each crystal. The design is often based on Sacred Geometry and the basic patterns of life.

Crystal grids can be designed and used for virtually any purpose. When the crystals are arranged properly, their energies are combined, amplified, and supported. Therefore your intention and specific needs can become focused and expands.

Why Do You Need Crystal Grids?

A piece of crystal can be a potent source of energy that will have a lot of purpose when prepared and used the right way. However, there are some cases when you feel like you will need more crystals to make your intentions manifest. But combining several crystals and knowing what each one is for can be quite confusing. Arranging them the right way so that their energies will complement instead of clash with each other can also be quite difficult to understand. Crystal grids help resolve this issue!

When a crystal grid is constructed the right way, you will be able to harness the energies of the crystals effectively and easily. You will also don't need to worry about whether the energies are conflicting, or whether the crystals are arranged in a way that diminishes their powers. Instead, you will be able to use your crystals with strength, power, and confidence!

What Is Sacred Geometry?

The universe is infinitely complex and exceedingly simple at the same time. Everything in existence is composed of energy and matter that is built on a few fundamental design elements. There are several basic shapes and patterns of life that repeat in a seemingly endless combination of circles, squares and triangles that produce spheres, cubes, tetrahedrons and other 3-D forms. These patterns can be found on scales from molecular lattices to celestial galaxies.

Why Would I Need To Use Multiple Crystals? Can't I Just Use One At A Time?

Of course there are times when you could just use one crystal, and a grid isn't necessary. However, there are other times when you need more and you would want to construct a crystal grid. Grids offer a different type of energy that cannot be found in a single crystal. A grid is especially useful for when your intention needs a lot of power behind it in order to attract it to you.

Useful Crystals for Crystal Grids

There are crystals that are so versatile that they can be used in many different Crystal Grids, over and over again. They offer the most value for money long term and are a worthy investment if you wish to do more crystal gridding.

One Clear Quartz Standing Crystal Point

For most Crystal Grids you will need a crystal that is placed in the center. This is the Central Stone, also known as the Focus Stone. You could see this like the energy hub of your grid, it also focuses the intention behind it. It can be made of any type of stone and be in different shapes and forms. Clear Quartz is all purpose so having a Clear Quartz Central Stone means you can use it for any Crystal Grid. They are very useful crystals for Crystal Grids as they can substitute any Central Stone that you read about in my blog posts, books or through other sources.

Components

Grids use a number of standard parts that, when combined with knowledge and skill, can produce a powerful, synergistic combination of crystal energies. There are some guidelines to follow when combining and placing crystals for optimal results. Knowing which crystals to use, and where to place them on which grid pattern requires knowledge of the energies of crystals and of the universal patterns of life.

- **The Path** is the map of energy flow within the grid.
- **The Design** is selected to provide an energy path that is consistent with the objectives of the grid.
- **The Visuals** include design, color, and words or pictures that enrich the aesthetic and feeling you get when you encounter the grid.
- **The Elements** are the actual crystals including the Focus Stone, the Way Stones, the Spirit Stones, the Desire Stones, and the Perimeter.
- **The Wand** is a tool you use to activate the Grid.

The Path

The path is pretty straightforward. This is the path that energy flows throughout the grid. A well designed grid will have a clear path for energy to follow so that it can be gathered and focused into one point.

The Design

There are many designs that are useful for building grids. Many designs are based on Sacred Geometry and utilize basic shapes and forms. You can download and print all of these designs and several others as well in the Mumbles & Things Resource Library.

- **The Circle** - completeness, singularity, origins, divine will, unity, inclusion, purposeful action, new beginnings.
- **Vesica Piscis** - bring together opposites, bridge misunderstandings, connect spirit to body, unite divided things, healing emotional wounds.

- **Tripod of Life** - balancing, centering, uniting, stability, uniting groups of three (mind/body/spirit, past/present/future, maiden/mother/crone, self/relationships/career, etc.)
- **Seed of Life** - complete a task or goal successfully, harmony, balance, sincerity, truth, all-purpose grid.

The Visuals

You can enhance the aesthetic appeal of your crystal grid using certain visual features. The design ideas discussed above are just one visual aspect, below are several other ideas.

- **COLOR:** Use the color of the crystals to form patterns, or incorporate color in some other way to align with the purpose (flowers, images, colored text, candles, etc.).
- **VISION BOARD:** Build your grid on top of your vision board, or a vision board designed for whatever the purpose of the

grid serves. Use pictures of health and wellness, wealth and prosperity, happy and loving relationships, or the career or lifestyle you want.

- ☐ **AFFIRMATIONS:** Write an affirmation specifically for the purpose of your crystal grid to draw the intention into the physical realm and support the efforts of the grid.

The Elements

There are also several elements involved in the creation of a crystal grid: The focus stone, the way stones, the spirit stones, the desire stones and the perimeter. Choose all of the crystals in your grid based on their ability to focus and amplify the energy from your spiritual source for your specific purpose. This decision will depend on the crystals color, influence, and shape.

Focus Stone

The Focus Stone is crystal or stone that is placed in the middle of a crystal grid. Its purpose is to collect, focus, and magnify the energies in your surroundings as well as the universal life force so that it can be channeled into your crystal grid.

The Focus Stone gathers the energies and draws them down toward the crystal grid, creating a downward flow of coherent energy. The energy that radiates from the Focus Stone is shaped and modified by its color energy and the layout of the crystal grid.

Way Stones

Way Stones are the crystals and stones that surround a center stone located on The Path. They are very important in a crystal grid because they further modify the energies from the Focus Stone. They amplify and modify the energy flow that's entering the crystal grid.

Desire Stones

Desire Stones can be found in the outermost area of a crystal grid. They signify the desire, goal, or intention that you want to achieve by creating the crystal grid. Desire Stones are also energy gatherers. They gather the energies that have been focused and modified by the Focus and Way Stones as well as The Path. They give the universal life force energies their final shaping and fine-tuning to the desired result or outcome of the crystal grid. Desire Stones are also chosen the same way you would your Way Stones. You choose them by their color rays and crystal energy lattice.

Desire Stones are the crystals that you often use on their own to help you accomplish or achieve something. But using multiple crystals or feeding them with amplified and focused energies will make them more powerful to serve their purpose.

The Path

The Path is the line of energy that courses through the crystal grid, directing the energies from the Focus Stone to the Way Stones and to the Desire Stones. The Path signifies the journey you must embark on to achieve the desire that you seek. It's derived from the grid shape, which has specific powers and meanings. There are many designs to choose from when making a crystal grid, including squares, circles, triangles, pentagons, hexagons, and spirals. The Seeds of Life, Flower of Life, Borromean Rings, the Eye of Horus, and many others are also very useful and powerful grid designs.

The Visual

If you want to create a crystal grid that will help you achieve robust health and physical vitality, it's best to have a Visual of yourself engaging in vigorous activities and exhibiting good health. If you want to create a crystal grid that will increase your wealth and abundance, it will be greatly enhanced by a Visual of money or all the material things that you desire. The same can be said for crystal grids for love, family, or career.

The Wand

A wand is used to activate the grid. Draw the direction of flow and allow your mind and your intentions to connect the energy path of the grid. There are many different options for your wand. There are places where you can purchase one, however, it can be very magical to make your own.

- A small twig from a tree, especially if it's a tree with magical properties similar to the grids purpose.
- A crystal or several attached to the end of a stick. Quartz crystal is generally used for this purpose but it can be useful to use the same crystal as the ones you are using for your Desire Stones.
- Your own index finger.

Constructing the Grid

Now that you understand all the components of a crystal grid you can create one for your own purposes and desires. Follow these simple steps.

STEP 1 - DETERMINE YOUR INTENTION

We've talked a lot of intentions before. It must be specific and clear. And it should be presented in the present tense.

STEP 2 - CHOOSE YOUR GRID DESIGN

The second step is to match the intention and objective of the need to the various designs of grids.

STEP 3 - CREATE THE VISUALS

Use pictures if your desire is tangible. If it's more abstract, use affirmations. The visuals can also include a print out of the design you chose in step two. At this step you can start thinking about a color scheme as well that harmonizes with your intention.

STEP 4 - SELECT THE DESIRE STONES

When deciding on the stone you want to use, start from the outside and go in. The Desire Stones are often the easiest to select because they are the most connected with your intention. Pay attention to the color as well if you chose a pallette during step three.

STEP 5 - SELECT THE SPIRIT STONES

If you are seeking spiritual help and guidance select the Spirit Stones after selecting the Desire Stones.

STEP 6 - SELECT THE WAY STONES

The Way Stones require a more scientific approach to select because they amplify, remove obstacles and generally show you the way. Ask yourself what steps need to be completed to get from point A to point B and what challenges you may face on the way. Then choose Way Stones with energy that aligns with this or are a color attuned to the answer.

STEP 7 - SELECT THE FOCUS STONE

The Focus Stone collects, aligns, and focuses the source energy in order to bring its healing, life-giving properties to your grid. Choose stones with the ability to do with. Shape and size are also things to consider. Often times it's best to select this stone based on what feels right. Try several options and it will be clear which one to use.

STEP 8 - SELECT THE PERIMETER

This of the perimeter as the walls of a castle: containing and protecting. Crystals that are known for protection are a good place to start when building the perimeter.

STEP 9 - DECIDE ON THE LOCATION

The location is important, especially if you want the grid to stay up for several days. Energy should flow freely in the space you choose, so under the bed or in a closet are not good choices. Consider pets and children as well when deciding on the location.

STEP 10 - ASSEMBLE YOUR GRID

Begin laying out crystals according to the design and elements you have chosen. You may wish to align your grid with the magnetic field of the earth as if it were a compass.

STEP 11 - ACTIVATE YOUR GRID

Activate the grid using your wand. Connect your intention to the energy path within the grid by tracing the path of energy flow. Close your eyes and connect to your spiritual sky boss through whatever meditation technique you prefer. Pull the energy from the universe inward and allow it to flow through the tip of the wand into the Focus Stone. Visualize it traveling to and activating the Way Stones, Spirit Stones and out to the Desire Stones. The grid is ready to assist you in your desire!

STEP 12 - RECEIVE YOUR DESIRE

Realign yourself as someone who has already received their desire. Visualize yourself having what you want and feel the emotions associated with this.

There are many intentions and goals depending on the person who will be creating the crystal grid! When setting your intention, make sure to be very specific because this will determine which crystals you need to select for your crystal grid.

If you want to create a **WEALTH AND PROSPERITY GRID**, you should choose gold and green crystals like

- Citrine,
- Pyrite,
- Aventurine.

If your crystal grid is for **HEALTH AND WELLNESS**, you should pick purple and blue crystals like

- Angelite,
- Sodalite,
- Fluorite.

Orange-colored crystals should make up your crystal grid for **SPIRITUAL AWARENESS** and **SPIRITUAL GROWTH**. When you use these crystals in your grid, they will also help you connect to the spiritual realm and protect you from any kind of spiritual attack. They will also support you in making a new beginning.

CONCLUSION

Crystals are of great importance to the well being and positive growth of humans. It is pertinent you acquire some for yourself, able to ascertain the one that will be more beneficial to you, learn different ways of cleansing, charging and programming them. I strongly believe that this book has done great justice on every information you need to know about crystals. Please read and practice and also share with a friend.

REFERENCES

- Working With Chakras in Crystal Healing: https://remedygrove.com/bodywork/Working-with-Chakras-in-Crystal-Healing

- https://www.infinitesoulblueprint.com/what-are-chakras/

- https://cafeastrology.com/whatisastrology.html

- https://chopra.com/articles/what-is-a-chakra

- https://blog.mindvalley.com/7-chakras/

- https://www.mumblesandthings.com/blog/crystal-grid

- https://www.ethanlazzerini.com/crystals-for-crystal-grids/

- https://denmeditation.com/crystal-charging-with-the-full-moon/

- https://entertainment.howstuffworks.com/horoscopes-astrology/question749.htm

- https://www.kilmaincrystals.com/kilmaincrystalsblog/cleansingcrystals

- https://consciouslifenews.com/crystals-heal-chakra-balancing/1179779/#

- https://meanings.crystalsandjewelry.com/how-to-use-crystal-grids/

- http://archive.boston.com/business/technology/articles/2010/02/08/what_is_the_science_behind_quartz_crystals/

- https://meanings.crystalsandjewelry.com/chakra-balancing-improve-life/

- https://remedygrove.com/bodywork/The-Incredible-Science-Of-Crystals

- https://cosmiccuts.com/blogs/healing-stones-blog/how-to-use-crystals-for-the-best-chakra-healing

- https://hibiscusmooncrystalacademy.com/pineal-gland-crystals-part-1/

- https://www.thoughtco.com/what-is-a-crystal-607656

- https://www.dkfindout.com/uk/earth/crystals-and-gems/crystals/

- https://sciencing.com/what-crystal-how-does-form-4925052.html

- https://www.sagegoddess.com/what-is-astrology/

- https://crystal-information.com/encyclopedia/pineal-gland/

- http://www.geogemsmineralclub.com/2018/11/23/7-types-of-crystals-structure-and-shapes/

- https://www.healthline.com/health/how-to-cleanse-crystals#water

- https://www.gaia.com/article/crystal-care-clearing-cleansing-charging-your-crystals

- https://meanings.crystalsandjewelry.com/crystals-for-astral-projection/

- https://www.energymuse.com/blog/cleansing-crystals/

- http://astral-institute.com/2535-2/

- https://chopra.com/articles/enhance-your-meditation-practice-with-crystals

- https://www.energymuse.com/blog/meditating-crystals/

www.ingramcontent.com/pod-product-compliance
Lightning Source LLC
Chambersburg PA
CBHW070813240726
48654CB00007B/324